She
Who Brings
the Rain

ELIZABETH MARTINA BISHOP

Requests for permission to reproduce selections of this book
should be mailed to:
    Elizabeth Martina Bishop, Ph.D.
    2675 West State Route 89A, #1100
    Sedona, AZ 86336, USA

ISBN-13: 978-1530579396
ISBN-10: 1530579392

BISAC: Poetry / General

Design by Artline Graphics, Sedona AZ, USA
www.artline-graphics.com

She
Who Brings
the Rain

ELIZABETH MARTINA BISHOP

TABLE OF CONTENTS

PART 1

Descent into Hades:
Hybrid Mastery of the Underworld

PART 2

Do Poems Have to Talk to Each Other Like This?

PART 3

Perhaps
You Should Have
Never Settled Down

8

DESCENT INTO HADES:
HYBRID MASTERY
OF THE UNDERWORLD

Umbrella for a Drought

Doom-struck, my lungs
Are shot to hell
I've never done anyone
Any class of harm
Never smoked a joint
My lips are smarting
With topsoil filled with sand
Brought out by a fevered land
Will she who brings the rain
Get down on her hands and knees
And get busy.
A single raindrop
Might soap my forehead
With love and yet I know
These days requiems
For most of the departed
Including withered plants
Have stopped my ears
And the ears of my cousins
I cannot manage a coffin
Filled with worms

Question the Bringer of Rain

she who is the bringer of rain
is the bringer of a full moon
harboring no hint of suffering
no bragging of sun
in blessing of moon
In hours distracting her
rendering her lazy
when with her soul on fire
some force might chastise her
for bringing to the fore
the furnace of discomfited desire
almost you can imagine her now
lying on the brow and breast
of hill and untilled meadow
in fallow furrow
in the way of a young calf
lying undisturbed beneath an orchard
whose flowers blooming in carapace
yawn and still the frame of leafy blooms
their shuddering petals
still undying in the wind
conspiring to unfold
a grey apron at dawn
in fullness of uncertainty
untying twin shale-grey skies
one from another
tell me have I asked
too little or too much
or too much of love's
muted passion for birds
for I too take dark comfort

in a star that shields
its swans from feathered comets
soft- helmeted sparks
upwind of where we are
why shield your face
from a far-seeing visionary eye
standing out as it does
loosening a preternatural god
from heaven's eventual prophecy
where I live now life's eventual story
the blindness of mirrors only beginning

Sorrow

Sorrowful though I was
I could not tell her of my vision
As a guest of winter's keep
Beholden to emptiness
Of migratory sky-compass
The sweep and swath
Of swatches of Canadian geese
Flying in dilatory unison
Threatening to derail all of us
In shuddering wings.
Detective to the rose and thorn
Yet undecipherable
As derisive alphabet
Of fire-filled Orissa,
Hidden in moonlight
Though they were
Elusive, I heard them then as shadows
Flying and hectoring as they went
Over Long Pond at midnight.

Leftover Crusts

Now as I searched
For whatever leftover crust
Remained secure or within reach
As obedient ruse of discretionary clause
Or as decisive or discursive acts
Of illusion or delusion's sinecure,
At best, how could I remain certain of anything?
Life appeared as uncertain as the sweet flesh of the mind
Falling from time's polished and blind undertow of sleep.
Precarious and alone, what could I hope might appear

Feathered Water

As less than irretrievably lost, the fictive and restive image
Of feathered water scribbling a map moored in mindless wind?
Stone- cold and etched in restive and agonizing gaze of winter,
Fated from the first, those wayward and derelict stories
Retold of Ovid, Faust, Mephistopheles, Socrates and the rest.
They too were thrown off track in devious artifice of hide and seek.
Marked by unseemly detour and devious pathway
To withstand the workings of the hooded furies kept at bay.
Now as the geese continued to divest memory's keepsakes
Swimming discourteously at behest of midnight muse

Impersonating the Muse

Make no mistake about it:
When one who dares mimic or impersonate keen and canny antics
Of a black swan caught off guard in a wanton moment of abandon,
Who surreptitiously lowers a veil
Or gamely retrieves or retracts her vest
At best, divested of its surreal ill-chosen conceit or boast
And endures or incurs ruse or rounds of jest
In ill-timed grammar of syncopated heartbeat,
What next does she encounter if she the one half- vexed,
Soul-tossed, half-surrendered,
Or sundered by ill-timed body's duress?

Self Defeating Muse

Unless she a person, when routed and rerouted in milk of defeat,
Mile for mile, moored in yard cloth sundered in its entirety
In silken-skeined palaver of interrupted words, its flesh and blood
Half-obliged to part company with heart after heart after heart,
Then is it so hard to imagine black swan
As toppled in her innocent demise?
What part of her that is woman is sure to wail and shout?
And offer protest in groundswell in among a pile of fallen leaves,
Heaped up and blasted in disused foliage of reprieve?
If love lingers at the breast of old age
Feathered the touch of lust remains in a chaste state of disarray
Undone, perhaps, chastised as well, or under-sung.
If beholden to no one and half-hidden
The setting of the sun unbidden
And absurd in the west, what then?
Though once we endured and suffered
Before the stolen tundra of youth
And half-plundered ghosts of summer and gossamer morning,

Beginning and Ending
of Story

Long ago, we boasted we knew or thought we knew
Of the beginning and end of the story, such as it was.
We might wonder then why we sang as long as we did and as well
Lingering in groundswell of fallen leaves
With the high notes in decrescendo and vibrato
Sounding into the hollow well and welter of hollering water:
The place where we fled and fell
Offering little or no resistance to a wedding of sound and sense:

Arguing at the Crossroads

Seems we can't abide, can we,
The art of congenial conversation,
Here we are instead in
Another half-completed incarnation as woman,
Arguing at the crossroads about our lack of a sense of direction.
Silvered the hair of the woman-goddess shouting at us,
Wildly gesticulating,
Telling us of another grammar necessary for braving another wall:
A replica of a tiny ocean singing salted at the moon tide
Of her dragon's breast.

Raven Chant

I cannot speak of him
Who sings to crows and ravens
All day and all night
As every turn of phrase
A star extinguished as a crown of thorns
He who resides in ink-filled clouds
Claims his feathered birthright
Serves only the eyeless brave
Forsworn to death dominion
Before he forgave breath as life
And life breath as death's charade
Debt-ridden

Among nameless grandfathers
Parading across forgotten meadows
Blameless as sun and moon
And wayfaring comet or meteor
Those as seekers who never claimed
What they knew could not be fed
Into mother turtle's rattle or gourd

Nor had they ever lived
Downwind
Of Mother Earth
Nor upwind of the stars
Whoever it is remains
Anchored or non-anchored
By stair and shell-spiral
Flies and never refuses
Death's amorous warrior cry

Poem for a Rainy Day

The second you try to die
Or kill or maim a spirit
And make it stick
Try living in non-being
For a momentary respite
And you know it's one
Second too many
In order to kick the habit

A canary is always given a second chance
But here the lettered or the unlettered
Feign imbalance as non-nonchalance
In chalice whose golden brim
Tethered to diadem
How can one save Mother Earth
Redolent in indolence of disease
And unease while the medicine of biography

Brutal as a Magnolia

Weeping in the glen,
The Bible of myself cannot recall any single event
Made more significant or singular, one than another.
Brutal as a weeping magnolia
Blossoming by the arroyo
An accidental wing of a hummingbird
Brushes past
Even the most sallow and jaundiced cheek
Lepered the consciousness of words
Spent and misspent
Lit and unlit
Accursed and blessed
White shell
Obsidian glass
The gloss of enlightenment gleaming
Who are those who refuse to be humbled
Why aren't they taken to task
When encountering
A summer of hummingbirds
What do you or remember
You lead I follow
I improvise under memory's skin
The sun remembers everything
Of our soul's improvident refrains
The ragged constellations of our dreams
As meteors slumbering fall to ash
The rules have changed for our existence
Only a few minutes ago I remembered
What heaven might be like
And in remembering, I let go of life

The Daemon

Trying to predict what it is we should do
To gain an anchor in our lives, the longer we live,
We live in bewilderment and fire-filled pits of torment.
But how shall we live? Still puzzled, we asked the master.
The master said: don't move. Just contemplate and forgive:
The interpenetration of the veils should be enough
Somewhat moved and o
The leaping salmon in the rivers are the ones
Constantly reviewing the radiant overflow of the sun.
In fact, the master added, the radiance of a stone
Such as a sapphire therefore will keep you preoccupied
For years at a time. *Midwives Gossiping in the Outback*
The Woman at the Blue Macaw, Soothsayer's Dreaming Demon,
All of these surrender hints as to creation's impermanence
Take, for instance, the title, *Diamonds in the Rough,*
The Shaking of the Barley, both do the same thing and then some!
Some what? we asked. Do not ask! the master answered.
It is love that eventually will take you to task with gossamer finesse?

Over Dinner

You meet a friend who admits
To tell you the truth: I don't believe in angels.
Been there, done that, never did. Paper bag lunches.
Chalk it all up to experience: heart to heart talks.
I protest for dozens of angels
Form a doxology for altars.
How could there ever be enough cupids to cover
For every garden gnome? Or well enough
Do cement renditions disown
Or obscure the thorn of cosmic crown?
To me, angels appear much
Like wild asparagus springing up
Everywhere on sacred ground.
How may I vex the most jubilant
Harbingers of Creator's spirit?
Is that what you think you're doing?
Watch your step!
Why not surrender and give it all up!
Being such a vehement nihilist
Continuing to imitate concave/ convex:
Unrivaled parallels without the wherewithal
Mirrors the next best thing
Closest to them: in the sisterhood of Mother Earth.

Ambrosia

If hung with flowers
When cherry boughs
Vanish in ambrosia's fray

In banister
In symphony of air
When rarest of bird song
Remains unheard

Drought-filled
In
Wayside
Of detour
Scorned
As woe-begone path

If wine-cask
Overturned
Taken to task
By travail of sorrow's mask
And billowing veil

Wait until tomorrow
When frail apple blossom
Flies in the eye of a brittle wind
By and by

Is it at that time
When lute players
And mandolin-players
Decamp

With a confederate bride
Belonging to someone else
Who had
No elocutionary synapse

Sweet love child
In travail of midnight's
Broadside ballad
Don't bother
Thinking of anyone else

Don't think of scaring
The bodhi birds from the tree
Don't think of taking me by the hand
Before an indifferent
War-mongering
Indictment
From an erstwhile friend

For all I know spring
Like burnished nettles
In winter's trespassed demise

Thick with briar and thorn
Blurred with blackened stem
Of coarse dreams
What sits on your breast
Like a butterfly
Whose wings
Composed of pupa bones

Confessing
Its most disconsolate
And innocent birds

Inviolate as blood

Having no say
Having no voice
In any of this

While the soul within
Continues burning
In unlearned sequences

Measuring small silences
Remaining unspoken
As our bodies
Blown about
In discourteous foliage
Of disowned silk

In the way
Of wrinkled leaves
Casting out
Dimpled crowns
Forgotten by
Hedgerow
Ocean
And primrose sea

In the greatness
Of carapace
And canopy of old age
Wolverine howling
By a waterfall

No one can discontinue
Or avow was not her chalice
Consumed
Brushing the fluttering
Pulses of the wind

Owl Harvest

Birds cry out in anguish among fallow fields.
Though this is not the hour for the magnolia and the willow.
I wait. I sit. I wait for old age to bring her scythe.
Before the turning of the harvest beneath the cold light
Of the evening star, thus far a newer demon is birthed
As winter warriors have waited for as much as this
Out of earshot in the desert of yearning for morning.
Though I might wait and linger among verdant hills
Where stillness spooks the bell-tolled hour
Even among most savvy of coyotes and foxes,
My future lulls its gospel music to the inner core
Weaving and spinning an empty stem from a crooked bough,
I feel I've waited long enough. Mantras are exhausted.
Furies have despaired of ever gaining new ground.
Blindly I grope for a vision in an aspen forest
Whose leaves have turned to russet then to gold.
If I must grapple with a deer, a bear, a wolf,
Let the owls spread their wings and be done with me!

The Kindest Bird

Bird you are the kindest bird in the world
You open your heart to the world
But if the shudders of a camera close
And you continue feasting and fasting on images
You have forgotten the point to our existence
You only gave Bibles to those already enslaved
Without witnessing those already slain
Stained by the auction-block

Crown of Thorns

whoever speaks
to crown of thorns like this
persists in thinking father sky to blame
naming what still nameless among
sun or moon or stars
as turtle rattles shifting
in momentary dance
in uneasy parlance
of warrior-inspired orbit

Ballet Momma

Ballet Momma knitting on the sidelines knitting a red scarf oh so long and so pretty and so beautiful for her little stage delight Ballet Momma so what do you with oversight it's so easy to keep on knitting day after today while her daughter's body is getting lighter by the light of a radiant bright shining star and you know it's true her name it's gonna be in lights I guarantee it yes I do and isn't it the god's truth her body and her aura is getting blamed for getting greener greener greener and tamed everyday remember those days Momma when you were my starry-eyed pupil yes my little pupil my little partner at the Dairy Delight yes the Dairy Delight and then you stopped knitting your scarf Momma and you no longer knitted at the Dairy Delight and the place ran out of ice cream and shut down and what did people do when the ice cream ran out and Momma we couldn't buy chocolate and strawberry and all those fun and delicious flavors at the Dairy Delight and then Momma you ran out of wool too and at the wool store you went and asked what happened why did you shut down I was knitting such a pretty scarf too but then she faltered on the last pirouette and so Momma what did you do did you shut down Ballet Momma did you hide behind the curtains and shut down?

Ruse

It's not about living for a long time
It's about living well
No malingering allowed
My mother said
My uncle died of the flu
So did everyone else
My aunt and my brother and so on
Unspecified causes ruled the roost
No asides allowed
No excuses
The failure of the tomato garden
Pillow feathers that make you sneeze
With discretionary clauses
When the priestess of the body breaks apart
The loudspeaker in heaven
Blaring, trumpeting the voice of god.

Devotion

Unless a certain man
Possessing a brain
Decided how to use it
To become the keeper of trolls
In a garden
Meant for faith-healing
Or decided to enter the madhouse
Of the heart
Without grinning
To chase after black pearls
In an ocean
To pilfer fedoras
And birch bark canoes
What a shame
Management stands
Behind
Everything he did
And yet the brain
With the lid blown off the id
Lacks a magnetic needle
Belonging to a compass
If an artist charged
With a duty
Love cannot fathom
Try watercress
For a sense of direction

Fable

A carafe of wine
Devout flask
For scribes and seers
Outside coyotes howl
Take off the mask
Long have I loved rivers
Every window
Lit in the dark
Joyce's life in Trieste

Chivalry

Friends gathered
At a barbecue
I knew all of them
For what they were
Grammar found wanting everywhere
Except in the workhouse or the almshouse
Within the ragged fires of youth
People at each others throats
For no new reason other than
A fear of barking dogs
My mother was wanton
As chivalrous as the fireflies in may

Purse of Emptiness

A curve of smoke
Could not betray
An occasional interest in a new body
A husk of barley
A husk of barley and locusts
All the same
To him as a museum of misfits
Explore Tacoma
Violets or lilacs
In summer
Against the backdrop
Of a white-washed house
And see what you get:
Himself impersonating
Himself
Nothing else

Income Divide

wheeling in the upper room
of meadowlark driven
and raven infested sky
a grammar of high-falutin stars

do these
appear any less beguiling

if logic and order
subvert chaos
somehow
revealing
a bevy of astrolabe-bearing
astrologers
gathering to
calibrate and celebrate
the beauty of the stage set
including the high wire trapeze act

what is it that transpires
in Sandusky,
Ohio
that is different
from anywhere else

where
from time to time
locals from the five and dime
and the surrounding
environs of the dust bowl
of America
gather in full force

hounding
fairgrounds
and race track owners

some signs from purveyors
of warehoused intelligence
appearing
quite full of
of laid back
operators
of fun-
house museums
bumper cars
some of which
scarcely stop and go
unless of course
you hit a moose

merry go rounds
weight-lifting
pie-eating contests
pitch and putt golf courses
and horseshoe-throwing
comprise this pawnbroker paradise

cotton candy
circus barkers
buskers
non-descriptive
roller coaster rides
Ferris wheels
improvisational
water slides
impersonating waterfalls
known by the jet set
as part of nature's

god-forsaken outdoor
theme parks

shameful
each one of these
seismographic
self-indulgences
exist
for rich and poor alike

what else persists
save Khachaturian's
musical
pieces devised for clowns
on loose-fitting Turkish pantaloons

still my fear
of falling
remains obvious
or circuitous
depending on ambition's wake

suddenly in an apparent about face
I lean
I pivot towards self-awareness
impervious
to crowd-pleasing events
like this
as superior acts of success
or choreographed events
including kindness

DO POEMS HAVE TO TALK
TO EACH OTHER
LIKE THIS?

The World Does Not End

I rejoice in the animal dark
A ragged moon
Invites a jaundiced journey
For imaginary gurney
The take away spirits
Have gotten their way
For too long
An absence of hope
Predominates
I bask in the stone sun
This philandering has to stop
Dogwood blossoms
Cool to a stop in a river
Rife with syllogisms
And blue sparks
Grammar of wild asparagus
Cares what happens to you
Almost
But not enough

Good Samaritan

she keeps hens
in a chicken coops
meant
for ferrets, gerbils,
or for feral cats

she fashions
sash belts
mapping inclement weather
with beads depicting pollen-bearing flowers
overflowing with silver stars
and great dollops of golden glitter

crystals she sells at the fair
dug up from behind
her front garden stoop

each one crafted to perfection
as she the one wrapping them
in cast off woolen sweaters
from Daisy's Dime and Thrift

using extra thin hoops of copper wire
purloined and pilfered
from discarded
drain pipes

she creates cheerleaders' banners
she fashions doll clothes from culottes and cut offs
she gives Reiki lessons at the local old folks home
she gives guitar lessons at the youth club
she teaches TEFEL class once a week

when she hangs out her laundry on the makeshift
laundry line strung between two privet hedges
people ask: what do you do for a living?

Market-Place

For crying out loud
my father said
nothing in life
is anything less
than derelict
or suspect

if miracles
serve as miraculous for mendicants
they are also boorish and unfair
to those of plebeian consciousness

before a fair-haired maiden
enters into the world of commerce
trying out for a number of bodies

before a Bodhisattva's vow
the world lies in a state of disrepair
and chaos and continues on the same

if that makes any sense
just look at the grammar of injustice
sprouting from indifferent hands

Herod's lack of conscience
martyrdom must inhabit and stir
the kingdom of remorse
and scattered incense
melt the hearse of self-indulgence

true love has nothing on
on concupiscent dreamers

everything that leaves
your hands
a lease expired
on a pilgrimage
mortgaged
to defray the cost
of contraband

a tax delayed
smuggled into a dictionary of wants
slanted descants of can't
and won't deride
the divide of derisive

still and all,
desire
somewhat pleasing
to behold
as covenant
even without
the presence of this bird
already bought and sold

Listen and Be Grateful
for the Wind

Thankful for the task
By now your eyes
Must see through this mask
You pull me by my big toe

Till I grow blind and deaf
And dumb with riddles
Must all of us now ask
During the Ides of March
How far have we come from home

Are we coming apart at the seams
Before a tailor has even been called
Or a meeting convened
To assess

Parchment-like the clothing
The nature of our preferred vestment
Convened by those scribes
Acquainted by the gist
Of paper runes

Although rendered invisible
Now the open road
More plausible
That lies before me

While my tomb is edged
With thorns and golden threads
Ransacked from another tomb
Known by scribes in ancient Persia.

At dawn I find much to my surprise
The whorls of my gnarled fingertips
Are blurred with improvident oversight
A radiant luminescence of a new sun
Gracing yet disfiguring
Wisdom's lean to now undone

Everyone who has ever tumbled
Down into great tunnels of bedrock
That proclivity towards darkness
Leading to Rome or to China

Must first admit he entered
A sarcophagus
From which he cannot return
And be almost human

This Island Where I Live

For a long time
I am one who has loved rivers
And pitched my tent
Alongside reeds
Sprouting
Among stone fables
Hyperion roots
In cahoots with claimants
Witnesses, masters, sages
There is still plenty of time
For searching left
Sometimes a beaver lodge
Makes things plain and simple.

Credo

Christ wears
A penitential mask of thorns
As well as the mirror
Moored in ghost-ridden shadows
Discarded by lovers and fools alike,
Who can confide with certainty in the same light
Thick with burrs colliding with windows
In the burnished light of afternoons discarded
Yet, at once, overlooking fields of marigolds
And ancestral birds shamed by flight?
While I stand in recognition of the great mother
Why am I still drawn down by a statue in the park?
As a traitor bearing witness to the goddess
I flirt with bronze and am much too much polite.

All the Words of your Body Must Truly Resemble Light

given the words
of your body
must come
from somewhere else
other than a pine tree
aflame and dancing
in the wind

words summoned
and welcomed
of their own accord
channeled
from the fontanels
of various spirit beings

such as dyrads and nymphs
penciled in
representing
picturesque
antqiue scrolls
coveted
by various salesgirl
angels indwelling
in multi-facted spiritual realms
don't belong to any one body

meanwhile those beings pitching their tents
among patches of silvery swampland
never complain about land of origin
even if they come from a different
time and space

so now you might begin
to understand
whenI spotting grey wolf pelts
hanging on rickety coat racks
in the market-place

a conniving darkness gave way
to the beating of an animal heart
marked down by Mr. Coyote
somehow that imitation fur
stirred and presaged outrage
within my soul

only then did I dare look
at my dog lwith less diligence
no longer embracing him
as a taxidermologist might
a specimen inspired
luminous with second sight

Find Out What Makes the Heavens Tick

Look carefully around you, please observe
How most animals seem to know how to behave
In an earthquake. They know what to do:
Ants and elephants behave the same. Humans
Alone stand out as they await a sign to tempt egress
Or dip their feet deeper into a sand-filled keep
Where bell-tolled waves once knelled an earth song.
All along humans want proof of externals and weep
Before footprints, crowns of thorns, swans, caverns
Pawning darkness for light. A carpet moving
In a certain direction, a handmade basket
That might refute the nurturing spirit.
When delight mistaken confounds
A parent of solitude, hear how humans
Praise a mound of stones where once a Delphic
Goddess spurned advances of a swain
Intent on the domain of prophecy's domain.

At the Black Swan One Day

Daska, why did you go and dunk
dark chunks of the thick
black bread from Odessa
into the cup at the Black Swan?

Who is it you were so very fond of
that you dared raise your cup to his memory?
Go ahead, invoke rain, hail, sleet, and storm.
Stained with the gluttonous blood of summer
you even bent back the hands of your children's fate
by giving them winter names!

What of the dorm rooms on the second floor
of the publican's house?
What could they possibly mean to you now?
Don't ever bother calling at the Black Swan again.

Now as you drum
your scoundrel's fingers on your writing bureau,
now as you stand back and stare at your dogs
continuing to nip and and to tug
at the vacant eyes of the gentry,
they as well as you only pretend to forget
where it is you came from.

Those who have held out for more poems
than could have been written in one century.
They have long since departed, haven't they?
You hug and hold to ransom the kisses spent
the last blasted cup of wine that brought you down,
you hug to your breast

like a diseased lover come back from the dead.

You only use the cup not as an offering
but as a lip to drown your sorrows
to blur the truth that rankles you in sleep
like the blur of a thousand burrs
blossoming out of reach.

Even today you persist in drinking
to the followers of gods who never even existed.
You keep on handing out paper flowers
in the park to paltry strangers
then too even to their followers.

Why wait at the tube station
for no particular reason
other to celebrate your love of life?
Will the ghosts of unreasonable men
come to haunt them again
with the illogical passion
haunting irresistible wives?
Are they nothing but lotus blossoms
adrift on a wrinkled sea of life still churning?

What of the bitter berry
on the bough of knowing and unknowing?
Are we all to come to nothing
because of your disgraceful soul allegiance?
Chelas, statues fingering rosaries
resist the rusted confines of the grave.

What good could any one of them do you now?
Is it they or you who could not forgive
your passionate affair?
What of the guardians of the Black Swan?
You never laid a wreath at the tomb

of the unknown soldier on any account?
How many prominent warriors have fallen
because of your more conspicuous absence?

Yes, I know, I know, I know though,
you continually throw runes
and the I- Ching, and all manner
of instruments that might doctor your faith,
has there been anything that
could save you from yourself?

Were you ever saved by the memory of the dancing flames
spitting bright sparks in your direction?
What a disgrace you were to all you
who thought they knew you before your eviction.

When you came back from Odessa,
you were fired by the teachers of Druids
whom you pretended not to know.
Everything that occurred,
not the fault of anyone else.

Though your boss set you out to pasture
long before and made you wait with an umbrella
for the townspeople to notice,
since you had been evicted from your house of shame,
where could you go?

The boss man, he turned me out.
Is that what you wanted to tell all your friends?
You did not say.
Instead you said
I choose to remain silent.

When paramedics were called you cursed
the distance between anyone who offered

to say nothing because they took after you.

What is the nature of love that you live and let live
yet one more day?

Is it that the the sea has not yet
learned the art of perfecting waves,
or is it she does not dare to rise
without exploding into fragments,
those ligaments, the subtle arguments
of her former self?

Have You Forgotten Your Feral Cat?

O feral cat
left out in a fallow field
what suffering
among bulrushes
what does suffering
hope to gain
lunging into
furtive underbrush
that feral cat
takes so long
to admit
it is not he
but she who brings
the rain
a body
no longer a shadow
by reign of Demeter's Poseidon.

In the School House of Women

their shadow-ridden
paradigms of coupling
serving as exemplary fetish
of fear-mongering belief systems
hath caused me great pain
for which there can be no kaddish
nor forgiveness
not goosebumps
flowering
enmeshed in bouts
of piteous self-blundering
in a late tide
moon-driven
and unguessed
not the chill fever of illness
unsurpassed
in its bright Olympian star
blindsiding
nothing and everything
I have chosen for my life
according to the gospel
of the flesh
included this
my own persona
thickening archetypal wings
as irrelevant
revenant
forgotten
frogmarched

reinvented
caught in a standing room only
situation
an operetta
for which there are no new understudies
for "what ifs"
I knew before the night was over
and the curtain drawn down
the cat would kill the moth in the garden
I also knew before the next day was over
in the loose folds
of the hospital gown
would fall hopeless to the ground
this is how
rosaries
hung above a bedstead
howl and groan
before the tangled branches
of coyote's moon

Sur le lac de Connemara

Walter you emerge
from the shadows
the bougainvilleas
blooming on the front porch
on bended knee
you say
well here we are then
and then you ask me
how can I hold
a compass to my life
when the raven
has flown
in steepled rain
in another direction
where can I go where can I hide

university is more
important
than marriage
and the mail run
deciding the fate
of others
who deliver
letters
still remaining
unanswered questions
in a dark penumbra
and memory's
ominous future'
and besides
I am a water lily

Time

time
to start walking
again
and begin
looking into spirit-possession
all manner of possibilities for work
time to join the marine crops
or take a job
weaving chair backings
or one handed sash-belts
or running knitting machines
for displaced home-makers
I confess it's time to improvise
making nests
for wordless images
convening disembodied spirits
those birds
roosting in dovecots
making hay while the sun shines
time
to rinse summer clothing
time
I have no time
save to chronicle
the fact
long ago
circling the lunar tree
sacred to the Chinese goddess
I found was not the way
to invoke the angel Gabriel
with incense

After Spring Rain

This is not
a preacher's
ill-contrived sermon
or ill-timed
conversation
held in
a convenience store
of sorts

selling combs combo sandwiches
hair conditioner
native tobacco
gauze for after a tooth-pulling

a convenience store selling gee-gaws
meant for thugs
in various states of distress
over having no fixed abode

being enceinte
I know I did the right thing
I left the convent
and at high noon
I took the steamer boat
and fled to Liverpool

after marriage banns
were called
during a practice run
termed wedding
or civil ceremony

you dropped the ring
down the grate
too late to complain
to the nuns
afterwards
when we went outside
the courthouse chapel
on the park bench
to celebrate

with a hot toddy or two
you dropped the ring again
but what I did
I dropped the man
during the spring rain
and spring thaw

I dropped the man
and came to
only when
they found you
hanging
in the garage

you dropped the ring
I dropped the man
thereunto

ever afterwards
when I went to live
In Puerto Rico

Baltic Rainfall

she who brings the rain
is not a rain woman
nor even a consort
to a rain man
as bringer of rain
all she knows
knees
scarcely any kind
 of suitable
match for scrubbing stone floors
or praying
in between household duties
or bouts of love-making
try basket-weaving
with fingers
whose whorls
burned beyond recognition
try living this life
traversing darkness
nightmares
and the thunderous insults
of clouds
ready to give birth
any moment

she who brings the rain
longs for inclement
weather
storms
as an indictment
for having been born
as a breech birth
to boot
when all the midwives
were called
to birth someone else
so why should any child
long for life this much

who else could be born to ramble
to gather amber
in Basilica in field of insidious
and insolent and sullen rainfall
since black pods of beans
are hard as a corpse's birth
how can we end up
loving the same thing?

After She Brings in the Rain, What Happens Next?

a wasp circles
the room
before he's burned
blindsided by the sunlight
a thief of time
living on borrowed time
living in a screened in porch
one that is soon to be deserted
where stations of the cross
were once performed

are you aware I had
everything that summer
when the red-tailed hawk
failed to return
when before time
he never left his perch
and hugged the juniper bough
as long as he could

of course that summer too
was waiting
for the inevitable to happen

before the child was born
my daughter said
nothing will change
I'll make you lose
your job

who will take the bribe
to keep my hopes
and dreams alive

with that being said,
why then should my mother
ask after I'd given birth
is it a girl or a boy

all she wanted to know
and asked each of the hospital staff
before she went and rented
my house to a maidservant
from Mullingar who never knew
why she was gifted as she was
as a surrogate bride and daughter
to a hunch-backed crone

just look at you my mother said
and you the one
about to lose
everything you've ever loved
poor you you're not the only
one in the world who could not forgive
all that you ever loved you're about to lose
lose everything you've ever loved to a Polish Jew
a savant just like you

it was then

and only then I wanted to ask
was my sister truly
an exemplary
pegeen mike of sorts
the one
would spent the rest
of her life
harvesting
an ill-timed harvest
poorly defended
by procuring
alibis
for incipient indifference
by rescuing feral cats
already
feasting on the remains of serpents
delivered on platters
to Cornish game hens, pheasant
quail and ruffed grouse
such leftovers
full of splinters
serving as ill-timed reminders
of all those
thief-mongering
hordes of smugglers
from the coast
those who would eagerly
take out orders
used for sleep-overs
for prelates and such like

Love Poem

How can I face the next world?
Without you,
That would be impossible.
Sky would not seem sky
Earth would not seem earth
Nor the moon's eye
Half-opened
Would not shine like a jewel
Dimmed by the sun
An anklet bangle
Would surely
Break apart
As soon as I began walking
Across moors
Stoked by cairns
And standing stones
They would surely topple over.

When

when they told me you had left
I heard nothing
I was sleeping
ears-stopped
among sodden branches
leaves brown and green
branches tangled
and obscene

when the elders woke me up
I asked where have you gone
don't worry there isn't one of them'
I believe in

when they told me
I swore vengeance
on my tribal people
I stammered and stumbled

among singing bowls
I lingered in the temple spaces
of the mind
seeking the right note
borrowed from Baltic regions
those places where
all the notes are passed on
from one grandmother to another
one generation at a time

how could you have betrayed me
if I knew all of what you'd done
(and I do know)
I would no longer
dedicate
any one of these poems to you
nor would I feel inspired'
to recite my mantras
or perform the stations of the cross

when a girl leaves her place of hiding
every one of the doors
slams after her
tight shut

that lesser men
should not hold her accountable
for what she has done
which is absolutely nothing
save be born

for she has no part
in the cosmos

Enlightenment's Scandalous Ways

I sleep with pagans of daylight
I sleep in the blind willows of time
I sleep during brackish storms
Until my bones forget their money
I never claim to hear the thunder
Slip the silvered lightning's noose
You would have thought an astronaut
Birthed a baby star
For all the moon reports
If sound in a room
Abandoned by rivers
And crescent moons
As a lover single-minded
In the rounded sweep
In the contour of a single comet's fire
Your might hear your heart pounding
In the way of the loudest drum
Storm-tossed
If love can succumb
To syllables barely mouthed by children
In the grammar of logic's cryptic galaxy
All but drowning my mind
In the common tongue of impossible cosmos
That's where I am bound
I own with the next dirge on my lips
In exile.

PART
3

Perhaps
You Should Have
Never Settled Down

Inheritance

The old crone
Could never believe
I could make you happy.

Well, it's true
I can't.
At least,
You are not a liar
About that kind of honesty's
Brokered truth.

That's why I sing as I do
To the heavens
With the rants of the dead
With those quickened by the fire
Of terror and dread.

And still a drought remains
In California.
Who could say
That it's all to the good?

Winds know
Nothing of who I am
And why consonants
Stick on my tongue
As burrs on the branches of the land

She Who Falls So Gently Through the Boughs of Time

no one heard her going
a world absorbed in mourning
cannot wake up the threads of knowing
when every tongue in the world
knows a different prayer
and ignored the drowning
the barbed wire
and the innocent birthed
on a wave
why are we all slaves
to the different music of the blind
smothered in the wake of a wind
the kind of a wind
that never stops blowing
and whispers as yet a still born child
returns to heaven
you can feel that kind of passing
a long way off

Earthquake

They shut off the electricity
They chopped up the garden fence for kindling
They pruned the grass to near balding
They dowsed the flames
Of the gas lines
They disguised and disfigured the walls
No one knew
The village idiot
And the town crier
Told everything before
And tears were shed on graves
So that Odysseus
Would find his way back home
That everybody would be so lucky
The logic of fire and war
Less costly
That children would learn Yiddish
Instead of Homeric Hymns at school.

Maybe

If the wind knew all the answers
The wind might shout back
And make a clamor
A disturbance upon earth
Where a glittering world
And shining surfaces
Might outdistance love
And dark tendrils
Creeping from within a clefted rock
Painted with petroglyphs
Might refuse a wound of ink
The printed page
And the heart of thunder
Retract its wings
And roar
Growing feathered voice
In silence
Where music could never occur
To a composer's illumined scansion
Knowing grammar's width
Informing no time and space
No human face
A disclaimer statement
For those who sign documents
With an x
While inviting a kiss
From Heidegger's uncertainty principle.

Willow Branches

This week professional pruners have come
Announcing a time to celebrate
A lopping off of uppermost branches
Known to humankind.
When a man complained
About his privet hedge, last week,
Persisting as a misdemeanor,
A bird's nest he'd been photographing,
Became silenced by pruning shears
Later, he received a nuisance warning.
Picture perfect willow trees fascinate
Even the wind blending in perfectly
With vagaries of the local scenery.
After a marathon heat and a hurricane
Last summer,
My grandmother
Wept when her willow tree toppled to the ground.
She offered: how can nature be so cruel
As to strike down the last dancing tree
Remaining by the pond? If ever a god
Or a goddess were elected president
And were selected to watch over pain
And suffering wrought by she who brings
The rain, I reckon through all of this,
I'd be the first one losing my taste for life.

Don't Tell Anyone We are Liars or Why My Aunt Keeps Singing Songs of Total Disaster

who is she really
is she a witch a bitch a whore
or the ghost of a zombie relative
keeping score, totting up
how many leaves
have broken ranks
with a wind filled
with leafy shadows
brimming like
froth from other lifetimes
during famine, plague,
and pestilence
what of those lives
where we were so ground down
with everyone
love no longer mattered
guess today I'll hang out
with burdock and roses
and watercress
with sparrows and bullfinches
before setting
out each of my linens to dry
what kind of dry dock
is this soul witnessing

a hurried blessing
before the sun
has her way with me
may I have this last dance
later with tear-stained cheeks
guess I'll choose to drink
away all my sorrows with
a player piano
on the patio of my dreams
while the next door
the magpie agrees to cheat
on his wife tomorrow
and the two wrestlers
drink themselves to blazes
take a last look at the sky
before it falls

Who You Think You Are Is Not Who You Are At All You Are But a Changeling Child of Wind and Rain

If you think you are an empty shell
A husk, a shell left wide open on a beach
On a notorious sand dune in a mudslide
Or caught in a land erosion of some sort
Next to discourteous eel grass
You are right
Where all words flow together
As one
There you are as disconsolate ocean
When a party of djinn come dancing
In the front parlor door
Know this
Also you are the only guest
Who will announce
Without a loudspeaker
The time when they are to leave
And you the only willing party and host
To floors that remain unswept
Swept free of litter and refuse
What keeps us going on mother earth
Going going gone
Is there to be a drought
Until this game of chess is over
That is played out

And played every night
Under a full moon
Before the omniscient
And omnipotent presence of the Beloved
In the heady scent of musk and jasmine
Watch closely
As all the departing guests
Make hasty exits
Floating out the back window, each to each,
Disappearing into a garden of spirits
In a courtyard where Spanish jade abounds
Lapis lazuli persists
If love were to come smiling in your window
I would swim into a marigold mound of meadow
And come up for air
Only when you'd gone
And declared you were a minstrel or a wastrel
Absconded with your lute
Half way round the world
Why tell me
From the beginning
You never entertained a beggared thought
Of midnight or tomorrow's suffering
Instead you only gave false testimonies
Before those already engaged
And devoted to victories for widows
Encountered in song-writing contests
For the hearing-impaired, the blind,
The disabled, the maimed
With that being said,
How could you be so blind?

Ice Fishing

I hacked through frozen ice
Looking for a way out
There was no way out
My clothes clung to the bone
My pick axe turned to stone
Nothing new could I learn
About the habits of fish
Or wandering minnow schools
That walked
Beneath water's
Unwavering crown.

Commentary

People are dying like flies
Like locusts on a hunger strike
In camps meant for the damned
What is meant by this
Razor-edged wire
Criss crossing enemy lines
People are jumping ship
They want to know why it is
My little pony still brags
The brittle bells of a fragile childhood
And remains as silent
As a midnight moon
On arctic meltdown
Disowned. dispossessed
Disused estuaries of guilt
People are walking
On hot coals
And examining
The soles of their feet
As if they were
Animal jaguar pelts poached
Hijacked by smugglers
And their kin
You tell me
Where this poem is leading
I'll tell you where I'm going
And what's this obsession
With address?

Maggie's Thrift Store of the Heart

Among horses of the Limerick races
Which horse will come in first?
How do you like my hat?
I can't say much about it.
Can't vet the jet set
That's for sure.
Sell my house
Sell my wheel
Buy my love a sword of steel
So him in battle
He may yield.
Johnny has gone
For a solider!
I'm reading James Joyce
That's says everything about
Coaches, car crashes, hearses
And scotched investment ventures.
No one can quite understand
James Joyce either
The upshot of this author is:
Get your story straight
Now the stakes are getting higher.
Heart on fire,
How old were you
When you first thought the way you do
And became a writer?

Isn't it all about Romulus and Remus
Women running with wolves and the like?
Dipsomania, get off your high horse.
This velours pant suit goes great with your jumper
But not my Juliette's purse
That purse is becoming
Over stretched with faux-fur.

Pax Nobiscum

I am sorry
I am not contentious exactly
I cannot hear you
Can you address
Your compliments
To the wind
Or at least to some else
Within earshot
I am embarrassed
A little hard of hearing maybe
Can you unstop my ears
With some kind of ritual ceremony
Meant for those wishing to give range
To free-wheeling speech
That cannot fail
But to give comfort or solace
Conversation that cannot
Be misinterpreted by tribes
Or wastrels and those intent
On bringing some class of harm
On the heads of those
Classified as lonely, alone,
Discomfited
By pain
Can you come a little closer, please
Are you hard of hearing or what
What is intended by the mention
Of clear thought
Clear mind and that kind of statement
All those kinds of words
Indicating I'm just not

That kind of high-highfalutin' person
Nevertheless I am not an unthinking person
I am something else
Just blind
Someone else
Less certain
Yet seeking luminous thoughts of fool's gold
A patron of the arts with the a cane
I keep my options open
Though I keep my head in the sand.
When I start the car motor
I hear the purring
Of inebriate mountain lions
Drunk on occasions
During expressions
Where mountains yawn
With expansive possibilities
Where no one can trespass
Or single out matters of the heart
As an excuse for heartless attacks
Immune to the indifference of the human race

No Glass Ceiling
For the Muse
Who Failed the Mensa Test

No glass ceiling
For magpies
For maggots
For centipedes
Performing a drumming workshop
Down the hill
When a beloved priest
Comes calling
On the pretext of purchasing an indulgence
For Heaven's theme park
And instead speaks of death
Do him the honors
Run to the border
Gather up the crumbs of your life
You need to act grateful
For the sweet flesh of the mind
Is not yet an unkind tyrant
Even though all the church toilets
Have been closed and will frequented
By heroin addicts and thrill-seekers
He who saw through your eyes
For a moment and then let go
As if love of the imagination were no surprise
Seen through the story of no one else
In love with imitation's paradise

Keeping Track of the Joneses

Blame the black mold and the cellar gypsies
For what happened when on the stone stoop
Hunchbacked, fallen, I ended up as I am
Fevered, as a homeless priestess, a person without a cane
Imprisoned in paroxysm of darkness, thankless, lame.
Even as a prisoner of the light and in chains,
Better to go down in person as an honorable colonel
Feathering her fall in a duck-blind meant for princess warriors
Anything rather than as one outwitted, outsmarted,
Duped by the ignominy of the stage
The grammar of wayfaring hordes,
Bemused in the bedevilment of dancing brides
As a cotillion of aunts moving across the countryside

Better to sit down at a formal dinner table
Than one heaped up with condiments
With no rack of lamb or game hen in sight
Only later will you discover soft-bellied moon
Offered only its most yellowed linens
As eiderdown for those asleep
Notice, I've actually begun to tell you
What I really think about the arctic fox
The snow goose, love howling about the unmaking
Of the dreaming soul, the unfolding of omens and signs
Now and again, why should life take me by surprise.
I should have lied about every single detail of my autobiography

Umbrellas

brollies
I never carry them
I just let the rain
soak through
my grandmother's pockets
turned inside out
how many times
has the great river
sung of sorrow's mansions
in the sky
nobody has ever
caught sight of

who has broken
the cicada wings
of indifference
I view the rain
in the arms
of an impassioned
lover
who does not know
when to stop

good-natured
good-looking
avoiding
a neighbor's grimace
I ask this lover
for a priestly confession
instead mark of the devil
multiplies my tears

as interferences
why bother telling the rain
I need this drubbing
from someone else
I tell this other lover
I was looking for god
in the voice of thunder
instead this drought
found me out
friendless and alone
I muzzle the pitiful dog
named little lightening flower
mapping circuitous flames
as wind rises and falls
death worries at my heels

repeal the voices of the wind
deafen the ears of silence
embrace the storm
no self-defeating fear
in compassion's wake
no sickness here
no ominous voice
confirming
my mother's worst fears
now she clutches at her throat
for emphasis

I hear her crying out
you'll catch your death
if you stay out of doors

come-in-out-of-the-cold
my dear

as plaintiff of the dark
these words serving
as a kind of backward-looking compliment

in stark contrast
to what happened
when thunder split
poverty's speech wide open
and left me dancing
in stellar rooms of hotels
a good for nothing
vagabond with broken teeth
a minstrel with a never-ending hangover
when hunger pangs
drained my heart
of any sign of compliance
or competence
memory seemed to never quench
my thirst

Is She, Or the Moon Void of Course?

She pretends she is not dead
She pretends she is not as she is
And yet she appears as preaching the gospel
With an ill-practiced goosestep of someone
Else not quite herself frequented by torment
Lamenting herself, faultless words are set aside as evil
Divisive as the sting of salt in arguments among ravens
That testifies intensifying ignominy's swill
The tread of a footstep on a threshold's sill,
Unsmiling, spilling indecision's fire, a door jamb
A footfall of deception's dreadful witness
A tent whose withies, without compliment of a cloth

The Doctor Not a Poet

The doctor read
The fables of the moon
You're sick as a cur
On a lonely road
You need
A good Samaritan
He said.
Someone who is a fearless warrior
And has practiced yoga for centuries

A sensed a touch
Of muted arrogance
A sense of entitlement
In unspoken words

Nurse agreed
Pronounced a rest cure
Restricted walks
Healing procured remedies
Suddenly
As common as elderberry wine
And lemon juice
Or chamomile tea
In my day
It was brill cream
At this moment,
My daughter who is not psychic
Proclaimed
She was an avid vegetarian
But could still eat fish and dairy
And disliked wolf and coyote

Coats ransacked and pillaged
From Minnesotan distilleries
In Nevada, the Dakotas,
Or Montana

Coughing was the reward
For prophecy's far ranging badges
Of honor
Courtesy of well-traveled ravens
Heard in the distance
It was only now
A dream of prophecy
Began unraveling.
It has been stated
In some manuscript
Detailing proverbs
From Indian country
The grass is always
Greener on the other side
The other side of what
I want to know
Though children keep insisting
They know the contents
Of the packages and keys
That can open the pearly gates
And offer us insights
Into witch burning'
And the torture of the angelic psyche
If machines kept my mother from dying
My fear of flying kept me here on earth
You made the wrong choice

That's what I think
No longer can I keep it to myself
There is no glass ceiling
When it comes to the price of dying
The dying swan ate tuna fish while on tour
Because of the cost of rations
Used by inhabitants of Gorky Park
The price of incivility's detour
Once I dreamed of an alligator
Who crawled to the edge of a river
He appeared as a gladiator
Whose greed led him to swallow
A compass
A sundial
An hourglass
Leaning behind ragged branches
Of a jungle dense with riddles
Close-cosseted among the yellowed leaves
At least a jaguar awaits
Breathing those little jagged
And vile sounding breaths
A little longer than he dares
Awaiting for the perfect silence
Among curling fists of browning
Detained within a clearing
When the time is right he springs
Muzzling the czarina of cats for good
Although without a chain

Outrage

Relatives planned everything that would happen
In my life. A game of cards forbidden.
The taking of another woman's husband; another wife
Considered libidinous, adulterous, an impolite routine
To be held up before pagan idolaters. Meanwhile,
Things were not supposed to end up this way
Sequestered as a hand-picked Letitia or a Lydia
Hidden behind supercilious white-washed walls
Of a dispensary selected for wounded veterans
Of foreign wars, pock-marked within confines
Of an unforgiving and forbidding antique facility
A facility situated in the hills of Indian country, yes
How could I report on such a lack of repentance?
How could I live as a non-person, woe-begone, a prisoner
Belonging to no one family? If tainted that bright sense of justice,
That cracked star, not enough to make me fail the braille test,
The test for those hard of hearing, the infirm, the maimed,
Not enough to tender blessings on those who rendered me illiterate
An abhorrent savant, possessed by more than a dozen entities
Given no room for leave-taking or making my entrance
What beautiful paintings covered the walls
Of the interstices of my familial indiscretion!
No furlough for skirt-chasing, rabbit-hunting, chess-playing
Cris-crossing across the globe. No holiday for card-player
No days on which to celebrate the brittle yellowing
Of leaves in autumn,
The tightening of bones in the bondage of old age.

This Conundrum of Wind

Reform this riddle
With phrases
Swerving to avoid
Self-affirming life promise
Too openly
To escape detection by the muse
Revise your prophecy
Your category of blandishment
And forgery
Relieve, revive, reformat
Your unmapped tide
Of recovery's jargon
And paradisaical virtue
Illogical as a poem
Whose testimony
Chronicles revivified
In untilled field of corn
Until ransacked by thieving ravens
Stammering among hen-pecking magpies
Not received as hens at all
Yet those winged birds
Pillaging its grain
And if your daughter
The daughter of the moon
Not your daughter
Held to ransom by her husband
Or by the relative of someone else
Who never had a daughter
Whose fault is this

Unless the wind
Surrenders its misapprehension
Rumored in arpeggios
Convened in grammar of air
Among those indigent
And voiceless birds
Redolent with songs
Exiled by a gullible wind.

Lives of Marathon Runners

the child I once knew
if she's a zombie now
goddess god love her
truly the devil sucked
the spirit from her flesh
and left her for dead
on a balance beam
or in a field narrowed
by a frenzy of ravens
why should I be haunted
by her fear of death
it is unwarranted, friendless
spirit enmeshed in spirit
flesh entranced by shame

nameless in a field
heaped up with weeds
with the smoke
thorn-drenched
bracken-soaked

brought down
by a harsh wind
flawed the mortal tongue
that clutches at the throat
a burr to a dog's jaw

love that once beguiled
soft-bellied once her body's
broken keep
but now her eyes too costly
to trade for the dividends
of compassion's sleeping limbs
sleep therein or else the lack of it

what dims the complexion of a rose
or a mirror's fretful glance what survives
in the composure, the indolence of glass
a steady cry of murmuring birds
clamoring for ocean's reprieve
foxes in the glen keening
the shadow-player grieving
a dreaming cavern's deception

fracturing her surround
forgotten little bear songs
bejeweled with ancient fire
of chant and druid gong
if these that might have turned
her life around small trees
have awakened from browning leaves
what has denuded this hour
of solitude but loved deluded
deprived its surround

If He Teaches
Death to Acrobats

For all his days
He will lie cold upon the brow of ocean
A silver necklace
A sleeping tide of ice
From which deathly errands of injustice
Cannot retire its slap of waves
Tugging at the teat of silence and innocent days
Reviling all it has witnessed and chronicled.
What can revive him from the caul of a death sentence
Uncoiling from a noose of little revered silence.
The room of his mind is as cold as the medicine of the sea
That cannot identify the moon, the sun, the logic of stars.
I no longer believe in angels. or in swans
Swarming with of indifference
Mosquitoes have caused children
To defect to other lands
In an untidy exiles
From which their brains cannot return
Unless their wings singed
With with synapse of revelation
Still burning in effigy
Don't you see
There must be a larger god

In all this chaos
Larger than this one
Informing everyone
As to the process of transformation
Needed for the teaching
Of the chakra-ridden massesTo apprehend the hunger
Of the friendless, the lonely,
You have a style of weeping
That is not yet documented
By the winds of change.

The Handwriting
Is All Over the Wall

At breakfast, I stare at the wall.
I have a vision of the ocean floor.
When I smash a glass to pieces
By accident, you roar with indignation.
When you are joyful I grieve metaphors.
When you are sorrowful
I doubt the sanctity of the cosmos,
And the Spanish Gypsies from Barcelona.
Were I a malevolent spirit,
Lilith would never have wound
Herself around The Tree of Life motif.
Confessing I've lived incognito
Disguised all my life,
If no need for any of this indiscretion,
How long do I have to live inside
The prison of my body without a wife.

The Lawn Chair

With green and white stripes costs
Approximately one hundred dollars.
So did a painting
By Degas found behind the sofa in the
Second-hand furniture store called Cyclops

Gratitude

This the place
Where moving
You can settle in.
Where gratitude
Morphs into silence
And a measure acceptance
Where shelves coalesce
Moored in dark rhizomes
Before breakfast.
This is the place
Where handmaidens wearing clogs
Shake dust from braided rugs
This is the nesting box
Where dying to itself
Voice-ridden flesh
Makes no amends
Surrendering small gifts
Governing the hearts of great men.

Heart of Hearts

Is this all love has to say?
Parsing the grammar of the heart,
Crescent moon fails provide enough luminescence
To hold the science of our dreams in check.
Yet thinning presence of a shining eye
Does us such little harm, we are blessed.

Meteor Light

Had the deer come close
To clearing the fence
Before advancing out of the woods
Towards a headlight
He might have chosen to sit out
The feast day of another incarnation
Who then would dared sweep him up
Shattering wing after wing
In avalanche of days
Crowning a rack of antlers.
What a gas guzzler this car is:
That's all you need to know.

Back Pocket

You are the man
With a back pocket
A flask of whiskey.
A dollar bill.
A poet's book.
A pen a knife.
I know it not.
That time forgot.
But I have not.
Comedic acts
Of mercy.
You nearly got thrown out.
Of school.
Birds in a cage
Of summer sizzling.
We envied your clout
As students we envied
But I am not your wife.

A Fish Out of Water
To My Mother

Oh
Don't let the rain come down
My roof has got
A hole in it
And I won't drown

Or will I drown
In a torrent of woebegone phrases
A piteous downpour almost deafening
My surround. A blackbird pretends
He will outlive everyone else.
Owlets blanched wings
Coyote laughter,
Quail disappearing in underbrush
In Shakespearean asides
And leafy aisles.
Flesh cries out
For justice.

A prairie hen
Refusing to surrender to her children
Caught in a rain-soaked underbrush.

You said you must sort yourself out
Decide what is more important
Wandering in exile or poetry rants
Delivered cowgirl style on a stage of life.
You know you can't have both.

The pond at the edge of the wood
Agreed with you about what was good
And what not so good.
In the glare of sun
Meant for everyone else

I stiffen recalling those words
Might you not outwit
Quixotic foxes in the glen
The sweet stench of death
Soiling your undergarments

A blood red moon sickening
Blind-siding a relentless wind
Nothing will let you be still
Beneath a magical path-working
Hidden in uneven tapestries
Of a patchwork quilt
Stitched with lies,
Is there any substitute
For rain and love-making?

Drenched in the monotonous music
Of death's alembic,
Why do your black hairpins, bobby pins
Stand around end to end
Inside your medicine bag
As penitential remembrance

Chilblains, kidney stones,
All the same.

Frowning a heron
Stands on one leg
And then another
Refusing flying
To distant parts

In Round Pond
Sedge-sodden
Knitted in grey green
Mosses
Interwoven
In the wedding of remembrance.

Before you succumb to cancer,
You paint a portrait of a Buddhist monk
Calling him your brother.
Summoning forgotten relatives
From a long time ago
Crowded round your bed.

Rain is a such a blessing
You tell me now and again.
Such a blessing.
Greening fronds
And little bow-legged frogs
Unfurl among hems and diadems
Of serrated ferns

My mother sings of everything
That separated us
In this life and in many others..
But she is dead.
Anchored to earth's awakening

Still is still dead.
Dead to love
Dead to spring
And the lack of love in her life
The women in my lineage
Never uttered sounds
In their love-making
In their crying

When they became hard of hearing
Or blind, they hired servants
To do all the talking for them.

Rain Already Falling

This was not your typical rain dance, I told my grandfather,
Wrong kind of weather for that. Consider the plight
Of sky goddesses unwilling to be shacked up
At least not in the way of a tortoise detailed, detained, defiled
On the Galapagos Islands, drought-filled and stark,
Among scientists immersed in dark scientific realms.

Those who knew of my grandfather's itinerant ghost
Often summoned to watch TV sets
Until the caterwauling agents of daily news reports
Left town once and for all. If told what to do, my grandfather
Often resisted that little bit of caution. Often he was heard praying:
Angels, you need to protect me as I roll from beneath satin sheets
Belonging to several servants of lovers, not just one or two.

In the olden days, among trysting harems, on thimble-size
Movie screens filled with craw-fish eyes of betrayals,
When a scheming Marilyn left Gregory for George
And Gregory steadfastly refused to abscond
With someone else, evidently, it was already raining on the stage set.

Since I had wanted to go further in love-making than in the past,
I used only the choicest of old-fashioned typewriters to get by.
In a typical dalliance in the mythical midnight air of dreaming,
In the ragged foliage of an old age encounter hosted by an airline,
I leased my house, I struck out for the beaches
Of the Pensacola Coast.

The Butterfly

The butterfly
Inside a cotton-lined case
Pinned to the wall.
Nowhere to go.
Memory erased.
Flowers everywhere
I've been waiting long enough.
Assume nothing
Of a warrior's grace

About author
Elizabeth Martina Bishop Ph.D

Elizabeth Martina Bishop writes prose poems, prose, essays and short stories and is currently undergoing the acquisition of a second doctorate in women and spirituality at CIIS/ San Francisco. She also blogs for Patheos.com, a religion and spirituality site.

Previous to that, she acquired her third MFA at CIIS under the tutelage of Carolyn Cooke. She also appeared in the San Francisco Litquake in 2012.

Bishop has her books on sale at Amazon.com and sells direct at various fairs around the country.

Interested in developing poems for the stage and developing her skills as a playwright, she has produced seveal verse plays and monologues.

Please visit her website at www.ElizabethMartinaBishop.com to view a recent selection of her work as well as the "Poem a Day" selection. In addition, she has published more than 50 collections of poetry.

Books by Elizabeth Martina Bishop

Elizabeth has published close to 50 poetry collections.

Here is a small selection of her work.

The Goddess Lives at the Columbus Caffe

These photos and poetry gathered here reflect the creative bridge in communication alternating between meditative image and the power of words.

The life of the bohemian poet is revealed, the aesthetics of image is reproduced for your enjoyment in order to
jump start the reader's imagination.

ISBN-13: 978-1511473569
ISBN-10: 1511473568 • $11.95

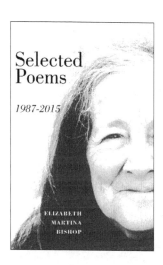

Selected
Poems

The poems in this collection represent a distillation of Bishop's works and showcase her sense of humor, as well as her whimsical approach to the art of writing poetry. While the parameters of her wide ranging poetic style are influenced by 'sound poetry' and her affection for performance art, she stands in favor of the idea that poetry may return us to a spiritual place that invokes a ravishing journey of inner awareness, peace, and soulful contemplation.

ISBN-13: 978-1507527849
ISBN-10: 1507527845 • $25.25

Words Not Yet Spoken

These photos and poetry gathered here reflect the creative bridge in communication alternating between meditative image and the power of words.

The life of the bohemian poet is revealed, the aesthetics of image is reproduced for your enjoyment in order to jump start the reader's imagination.

ISBN-13: 978-1505863673
ISBN-10: 1505863678 • $9.95

Tunnel Vision

Tunnel Vision expresses a kind of open and reverent supplication before Mother Earth's wintery and windswept altars. Elizabeth Martina Bishop certainly welcomes the chance to spread out her wings as we humans must try to endure climate change.

What if poets did not possess umbrellas and overcoats? So many people succumb to the numbing cold of winter; yet in extremes of temperature, many find a kind of a peaceful way of life without feeling lost.

Knowing each snowflake is an entirely different jewel may be the start of a new poem.

ISBN-13: 978-1505460551
ISBN-10: 1505460557 • $10.99

Made in the USA
Charleston, SC
12 April 2016